THOSE
FABULOUS
AMPHIBIANS

SIKORSKYS OVER BORNEO.

Osa and Martin Johnson enroute to
photograph big game. Pilot Vern
Carstens flying the S-38B "Osa's Ark";
S-39B "Spirit of Africa".

THOSE
FABULOUS
AMPHIBIANS

A PICTORIAL HISTORY OF AMERICAN AMPHIBIAN AIRCRAFT

DON C. WIGTON

HARLO PRESS / DETROIT, MICHIGAN

THIS BOOK IS DEDICATED
TO THE CHAMPION OF CHAMPIONS IN AEROBATIC FLYING,
A VERY FINE MAN WHO GAVE HIS LIFE
WHILE TESTING A NEW AEROBATIC AIRPLANE,
HAROLD A. KRIER

FOREWORD

It has been a distinct pleasure to work with Mr. Wigton during the production of this book.

After examining the material, the reader will be readily aware of the hours of painstaking research and the numerous persons that had to be contacted, letters that had to be written, and places visited in order to assemble data as diverse as that presented here.

The author approached his work as a good detective might, following lead after lead until he tracked down a particular photograph or necessary data.

Another fact that made the work pleasurable, was that it brought back memories or near memories to the individuals working at our press.

William Ortwine, who is responsible for the high quality of reproduction of the photographs (remember some of them are over sixty years old), is head of Harlo's camera and platemaking department. He was a World War II Army combat pilot and flew his own civilian plane for many years.

I was perhaps a bit closer to the amphibians because I flew the non-amphibious versions of the Consolidated PBY (illustrated on the jacket and inside the book), and the Martin PBM, also illustrated in the book.

L. W. Mueller, Publisher

NOTAM

THIS BOOK ILLUSTRATES
THE VARIOUS DESIGNS OF AMPHIBIAN AIRCRAFT
THAT WERE DESIGNED AND BUILT
ONLY IN THE UNITED STATES.

ACKNOWLEDGMENTS

My sincere appreciation to the following individuals, manufacturers, U.S. Armed Services and News Services that have contributed their technical data and illustrations in order to make this book possible:

Acme News, Associated Press, Ray Applegate, Earl Anderson, Gil Baker, The Bird Corporation, Peter M. Bowers, the Budd Company, Convair Corporation, Douglas Aircraft Company, Fairchild Aircraft, Federal Aviation Administration, Ford Motor Company, Frakes Aviation, Fred G. Freeman, E. H. Fulton, Grumman Aircraft and Engineering Corporation, Gus Hanke, Howard Heindel, Harold Hoekstra, Volmer Jensen, Lake Aircraft Company, Grover Loening, Leroy P. Lopresti, the Martin Company, McKinnon Enterprises, National Air and Space Museum, Piper Aircraft Company, Republic Aviation Corporation, Charles F. Rocheville, Alexander DeSeversky, Sikorsky Aircraft Company, P. H. Spencer, Molt Taylor, David Thurston, Gilbert Trimmer, U.S. Air Force, U.S. Air Force Museum, U.S. Navy.

—D.C.W.

CONTENTS

THOSE
FABULOUS
AMPHIBIANS

AMERICAN AMPHIBIAN

Information, including year of manufacture and technical data for this amphibian aircraft, could not be located.

AMPHIBIANS, INC.

1932

The Privateer III, a three-seater, pusher job, sold F.O.B. Roosevelt Field for $8,920. Amphibians, Inc., was formerly known as "Ireland Aircraft, Inc. The Privateer's engine, mounted on a tripod, was a unique way to install a power plant. The fuel and oil tanks are in the nacelle.

```
Engine .................................... Continental, 215 hp
Span ........................................... 42'5"
Length ........................................... 30'
Cruising Speed ................................. 100 mph
Maximum Speed ................................. 120 mph
Gross Weight ................................. 2700 lbs
Range ...................................... 400 miles
```

15

ANDERSON EA-1 KINGFISHER

1971

Designed and built by Captain Earl Anderson in his spare time, this Boeing 707 pilot took nine years to build the Kingfisher, spending $5,500 on the project. This is a two-seater. The windshield is from a Piper Tri-Pacer. It also has a standard Piper J-3 wing.

```
Engine . . . . . . . . . . . . . . . . . . . . . . . . . . . . . . . . . . . . . Continental, 100 hp
Span . . . . . . . . . . . . . . . . . . . . . . . . . . . . . . . . . . . . . . . . . . . . . 36'1"
Length . . . . . . . . . . . . . . . . . . . . . . . . . . . . . . . . . . . . . . . . . . . 23'6"
Cruising Speed . . . . . . . . . . . . . . . . . . . . . . . . . . . . . . . . . . . 85 mph
Fuel Capacity . . . . . . . . . . . . . . . . . . . . . . . . . . . . . . . . . . . . 20 gals
```

APPLEGATE

1940

Designed by Ray Applegate when he was engineer for Piper Aircraft at Lock Haven, Pennsylvania, this little two-seater, pusher, had a set of Piper J-3 Cub wings.

Engine .... Continental, 75 hp
Span .... 34'6"
Length .... 25'
Cruising Speed .... 85 mph
Maximum Speed .... 102 mph
Fuel Capacity .... 33 gals
Range .... 500 miles

ARGONAUT PIRATE

1935

Designed and built by Howard Heindel near Niagara Falls, this sleek, flat-engine plane was designed to be produced in quantity, but the idea was scrapped due to financial troubles. The Pirate carried three people.

```
Span ...................................................... 42'
Length .................................................... 27'1"
Cruising Speed ........................................... 90 mph
Fuel Capacity ............................................ 40 gals
Range .................................................... 375 miles
```

AQUA FLIGHT II

1949

This executive looking amphibian with little landing gear outriggers was designed and built by Meredith Wardle. He had hopes to put the Aqua into production. Unable to obtain finances for this big project, the idea was cancelled. The Aqua had a seating arrangement for six people.

```
Engines . . . . . . . . . . . . . . . . . . . . . . . . . . . . . 2 Lycoming, 190 hp each
Span . . . . . . . . . . . . . . . . . . . . . . . . . . . . . . . . . . . . . . . . . . . . 36'6"
Length . . . . . . . . . . . . . . . . . . . . . . . . . . . . . . . . . . . . . . . . . . 29'6"
Fuel Capacity . . . . . . . . . . . . . . . . . . . . . . . . . . . . . . . . . 100 gals
Auxiliary Tank . . . . . . . . . . . . . . . . . . . . . . . . . . . . . . . . . 60 gals
Gross Weight . . . . . . . . . . . . . . . . . . . . . . . . . . . . . . . . 4050 lbs
```

BAKER BC-1-4 POLLYWOG

1968

Designed and built by Gil Baker, the Pollywog Number One, Two, and Three, didn't have the speed that Gil had expected, so he switched from a turbo-charged six-cylinder Corvair auto engine to a 180 hp Lycoming. The craft seats two, side by side. The designer is now in process of making the final change in the Pollywog, which will be known as the BC-1-5. This single-boom amphibian has flown to many air shows in and out of his home state.

```
Engine . . . . . . . . . . . . . . . . . . . . . . . . . . . . . . . . . . . . Lycoming, 180 hp
Span  . . . . . . . . . . . . . . . . . . . . . . . . . . . . . . . . . . . . . . . . . 32'6"
Length  . . . . . . . . . . . . . . . . . . . . . . . . . . . . . . . . . . . . . . . 24'9"
Cruising Speed . . . . . . . . . . . . . . . . . . . . . . . . . . . . . . . . 92 mph
Range . . . . . . . . . . . . . . . . . . . . . . . . . . . . . . . . . . . . . . 400 miles
```

BENDIX

Information, including year of manufacture and technical data for this amphibian aircraft, could not be located.

BIRD INNOVATOR

1969

Seeing is believing. Yes, this four-engine amphibian is a PBY Catalina that was converted by the Bird Company, manufacturers of medical respirators for hospitals all over the world. The Bird covers the world and is a flying classroom for medical teaching groups.

Engines . . . . 2 Pratt & Whitney and 2, 340 hp Lycoming
Cruising Speed . . . . 200 mph
Fuel Capacity . . . . 2500 gals
Range . . . . 3500 miles

BRAYTON

Information, including year of manufacture and technical data for this
amphibian aircraft, could not be located.

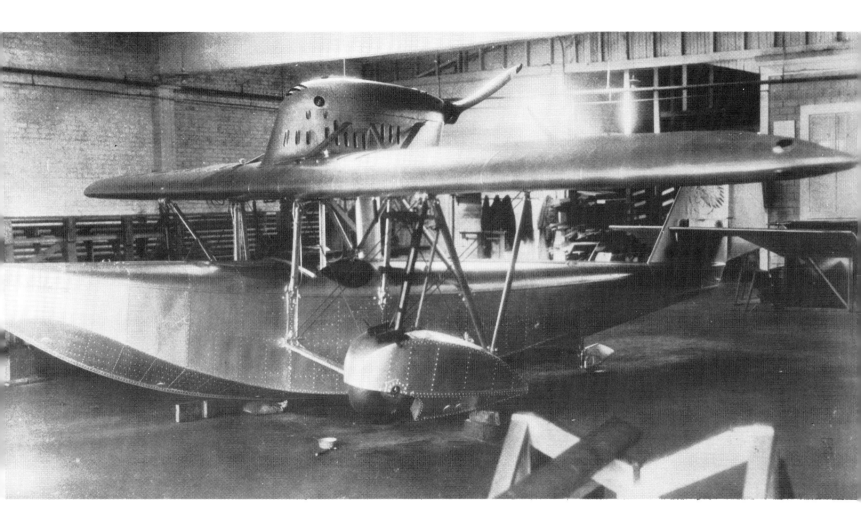

BUDD PIONEER

1931

This is the first stainless steel aircraft in the world. Built by the manufacturers of railroad passenger coaches and the Conestoga RB-1 of
World War II, the RB-1 was also a stainless steel plane and was the
Flying Tigers Freight Airline's first plane. The Pioneer is still in existence, but not flying. It's mounted in front of the Franklin Institute at
Philadelphia, Pennsylvania. It is an open cockpit job that seated two
passengers.

Engine . . . . Radial, 140 hp
Cruising Speed . . . . 80 mph
Maximum Speed . . . . 93 mph
Range . . . . 373 miles

BUNYARD BAX-3 SPORTSMAN

1946

The Sportsman resembles the Volmer VJ, only is constructed entirely of wood. It had seating arrangements for three people. This Sportsman is a home-built job, and only one was built. The BAX-4 (not pictured) has a 190 hp Lycoming, or can be fitted with an SH Cylinder Ranger engine. It cruises at 118 mph. The wingspan is the same as that of the BAX-3, but the length is 24'. It seats four people.

```
Engine ....................................... Franklin, 130 hp
Span ................................................. 34'4"
Length ................................................. 23'
Cruising Speed ..................................... 105 mph
Range ............................................. 450 miles
```

CADILLAC

1929

This one and only twin engine tractor type of amphibian of the late 1920s was flight tested near the northwest side of Detroit, Michigan. The wings were covered with plywood. The designers had hopes of operating this amphibian with two 150 hp Continental engines or two Hurricane 150 hp engines, but the amphibian, pictured, has two 110 hp Kinner engines. This airplane was experimental and later the firm scrapped it.

```
Engines . . . . . . . . . . . . . . . . . . . . . . . . . . . . . . . . . 2 Kinner, 110 hp each
Span . . . . . . . . . . . . . . . . . . . . . . . . . . . . . . . . . . . . . . . . . . . . . . . . . . 46'
Length . . . . . . . . . . . . . . . . . . . . . . . . . . . . . . . . . . . . . . . . . . . . . . . 31'3"
Gross Weight . . . . . . . . . . . . . . . . . . . . . . . . . . . . . . . . . . . . . . . 3700 lbs
```

COLONIAL SKIMMER C-1

1948

Designed by David Thurston and four other persons, this single-engine, pusher-job has a seating arrangement for four persons. The Skimmer was first flown in July 1948. When built, the amphibian never was wind tunnel tested, but proved to be a good flying amphibian.

Engine	Lycoming, 125 hp
Span	34'2"
Length	23'6"
Cruising Speed	115 mph
Maximum Speed	125 mph
Fuel Capacity	40 gals
Range	700 miles

COLUMBIA TRIAD

1929

This Triad amphibian has no connection with the first 1911 Triad amphibian that was built by Curtiss. The Columbia had a seating arrangement for seven persons. Windows could be opened by passengers.

```
Engine .................................... Wright J-5, 225 hp
Span ................................................... 49'
Length ................................................ 33'
```

COLUMBIA XJL-1

1946

Just after World War II, flight tests were run on this mid-wing for the U.S. Navy. Similar to the Loening type of amphibian of the 1920's and 1930's, it was, however, equipped for jet assisted take-off. The XJL-1 can take off in high seas. Wings can fold for storage aboard deck.

Engine . . . . 1425 hp
Maximum Speed . . . . 200 mph

COMMONWEALTH TRIMMER

1945

Just after the Second World War, the builders of the single engine Sky-ranger, a land based monoplane, designed this little twin engine amphibian. Though only a three-place job, it could have been converted into a five-place amphibian by lengthening the fuselage.

Engines .... 2 Continental, 85 hp each
Span .... 35'6"
Length .... 24'9"
Cruising Speed .... 115 mph
Maximum Speed .... 135 mph
Gross Weight .... 2200 lbs
Range .... 500 miles

CONSOLIDATED PBY-5A

1942

This amphibian was the lifesaver of the Pacific. Many a pilot that had to set down in the Pacific after his plane was disabled on a mission was rescued by the PBY Catalina, operated by the U.S. Navy. Many PBYs are still being flown in civil registration in the U.S.A., Canada, and South America.

Engines . . . . 2 Pratt & Whitney, 1200 hp each
Span . . . . 104'
Length . . . . 63'8"
Cruising Speed . . . . 120 mph
Range . . . . 3100 miles

COOT 1-A

1971

Designed by Molt Taylor, of Longview, Washington, this job can only be built from plans available from Mr. Taylor, so that hopeful home builders can build it themselves. Drawings show that it has folding wings for storage at home. It can easly be towed in back of an auto. The Coot amphibian is a two-seater job, side by side.

```
Engine .......................... Franklin, 125 hp
            shown, but other 100 or 150 hp engines can be used
Span ................................................ 36'
Length .............................................. 22'
Cruising Speed ................................. 100 mph
Fuel Capacity ................................. 30 gals
```

COOT 1-B

1970

This twin boom pusher amphibian is the third in line of water type aircraft that Molt Taylor designed. His first airplane designed for water operation was a single tail flying boat, having no landing gear. The Coot 1-B is designed to have folding wings for storage in small places. Although the wing span is 37 feet, with wings folded it is only eight feet wide. The Coot has a seating arrangement for two persons.

Engine . . . . Any 100 or 180 hp aircraft type
Span . . . . 37'
Length . . . . 22'
Fuel Capacity . . . . 24-30 gals
Gross Weight . . . . 1850 lbs

COX-KLEMIN CK-1

1929

This twin engine tractor type of amphibian was built on Long Island, New York, and tested at McCook Field, Dayton, Ohio. The engines were 250 hp each. The flying boat version had two Wright 200 hp Tempest engines. The CK-1 amphibian had a payload of 7600 lbs.

Engines .... Wright Tempest, 200 hp each
Span .... 58'10"
Length .... 45'7"

CURTISS MF

1919

Originally designed as a flying boat, a slight change turned this MF into an amphibian. It was flown as a sport plane. The cockpit had a dual control system. It took 27 minutes to climb to 5000 feet.

Engine . . . . Curtis OXX, 100 hp
Span . . . . 49'9⅜" Upper Wing
28'10" Lower Wing
Maximum Speed . . . . 69 mph
Cruising Speed . . . . 45 mph

CURTISS TRIAD

1911

This airplane, the first amphibian in the United States, was designed, built, and flight tested by Glenn H. Curtiss. Soon after the U.S. Navy bought the amphibian and it became the first Navy aircraft as the A-1. An exact duplicate of the A-1 is at the National Air and Space Museum in Washington, D.C. Though Mr. Curtiss had only one seat on board the Triad, the A-1 was fitted as a two-seater. The Triad is believed to have had a 75 hp Curtiss "O" engine. The Triad was first tested at North Island near San Diego, California.

Engine . . . . Curtiss "O," 75 hp
Span . . . . 28'8" (Upper & Lower Wings)
Length . . . . 27'8"
Gross Weight . . . . 1575 lbs

CURTISS WRIGHT COMMUTER

1935

It took about two years of experimentation before this five-seater pusher amphibian, designed and test flown by Capt. Frank Courtney, was successfully operated. The little mast pictured on the bow house is the nose wheel.

```
Engine ............................... Wright Whirlwind, 365 hp
Span .......................................... 40' (Top Wing)
Length .................................................. 31'
Cruising Speed ...................................... 125 mph
Fuel Capacity ....................................... 80 gals
Gross Weight ....................................... 4650 lbs
```

DOUGLAS DOLPHIN

1930

The first Dolphin was delivered to the U.S. Coast Guard in 1930 for coastal patrol work. Later the U.S. Navy and the U.S. Army acquired several. The Dolphin has a seating arrangement for eight persons.

```
Engines . . . . . . . . . . . . . . . . . 2 Pratt & Whitney Wasps, 420 hp each
Span . . . . . . . . . . . . . . . . . . . . . . . . . . . . . . . . . . . . . . . . . . . . . . . . . . 60'
Length . . . . . . . . . . . . . . . . . . . . . . . . . . . . . . . . . . . . . . . . . . . . . . 45'
Cruising Speed . . . . . . . . . . . . . . . . . . . . . . . . . . . . . . . . . . . 108 mph
Fuel Capacity . . . . . . . . . . . . . . . . . . . . . . . . . . . . . . . . . . . 266 gals
```

DOUGLAS OA-4B

1936

Out of the Douglas OA-4B, that had a conventional landing gear, came this one-of-a-kind OA-4B Dolphin, that was converted to a tri-gear for the purpose of pilot training for larger types of tri-gear aircraft, such as the Triple Tail Douglas DC-4 and B-19. The OA-4B had seats for seven persons.

```
Engine .............................................. Wright
Span ................................................. 60'
Length ............................................. 43'10"
Cruising Speed ..................................... 119 mph
Maximum Speed ...................................... 140 mph
Range .............................................. 550 miles
```

DOUGLAS YOA-5

This powerful Army Air Corps amphibian, the last amphibian built by Douglas, looks like some of today's sleek amphibians. There are seats for five persons. The craft could climb to eight thousand feet in ten minutes.

Engines . . . . 2 Wright Cyclone, 750 hp each
Span . . . . 90'
Length . . . . 69'6"
Cruising Speed . . . . 140 mph
Maximum Speed . . . . 160 mph
Fuel Capacity . . . . 700 gals
Range . . . . 1140 miles

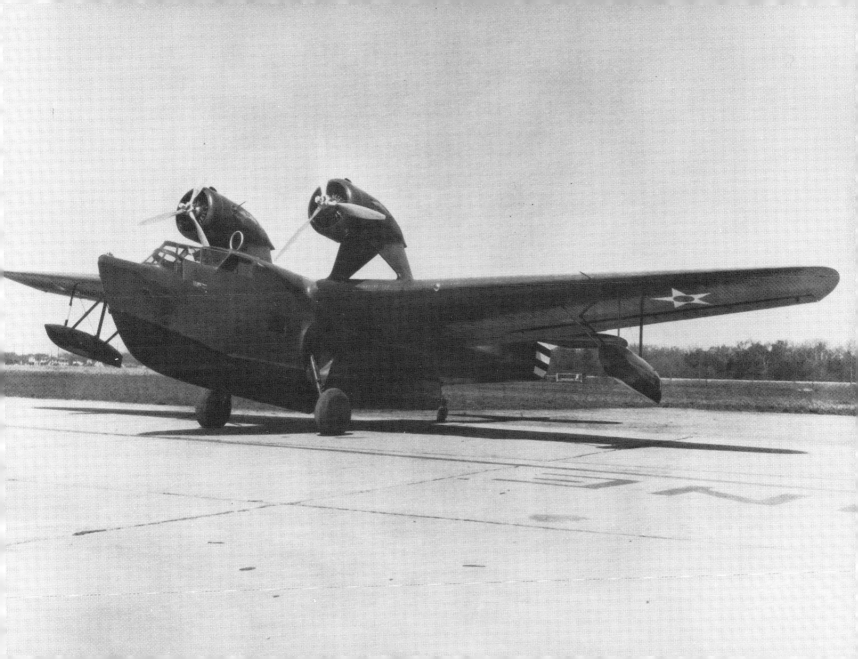

EASTMAN E-2A

1931

The Sea Pirate was first built as a seaplane, having no landing gear. Later the E-2A Sea Pirate was converted to an amphibian. This open cockpit amphibian had space for three people.

Engine .... Curtiss Challenger, 185 hp
Span .... 36' Upper Wing
                                             20'7" Lower Wing
Cruising Speed .... 85 mph
Maximum Speed .... 102 mph
Fuel Capacity .... 40 gals
Range .... 325 miles

FAIRCHILD BABY CLIPPER

1935

Designed and built for Pan American Airways' routes in South America, the little clipper was also operated by sports pilots and for company flying. The craft carried four passengers and a crew of two. Speedboat champion Gar Wood owned a Baby Clipper that had a three-bladed prop.

```
Engine ................................. Pratt & Whitney, 650 hp
Span ............................................................ 56'
Length ...................................................... 46'3"
Cruising Speed ........................................ 158 mph
Range .................................................... 750 miles
```

FAIRCHILD FB-3

1928

Although the Fairchild firm had designed other types of amphibians, the FB-3 is the first of an actual built-up plane. Most other blueprint ideas never got to the mock-up departments. The hull was all metal. The FB-3 was a five-seater.

```
Engine . . . . . . . . . . . . . . . . . . . . . . . . . . Pratt & Whitney Wasp B, 410 hp
Span . . . . . . . . . . . . . . . . . . . . . . . . . . . . . . . . . . . . . . . . . . . . . . . 36'
Length . . . . . . . . . . . . . . . . . . . . . . . . . . . . . . . . . . . . . . . . . . . . . 40'
Top Speed . . . . . . . . . . . . . . . . . . . . . . . . . . . . . . . . . . . . . . 133 mph
```

FLEETWING SEABIRD

1936

The Seabird is a true classic of the 1930's and there are still two Sea-birds in existence, one in Florida and one in California. It takes 8 seconds for water take-off without windy conditions. She carries four passengers. The fuselage and wings are stainless steel, spot welded. The only other planes that were stainless steel were the Budd RB-1 Conestoga, formerly flown by the Flying Tiger Air Cargo Airline, and the Budd Pioneer.

Engine	Jacobs, 300 hp
Span	40'5"
Length	31'5½"
Cruising Speed	125 mph

F 201

FOKKER F-11A

1929

Tony Fokker, designer and builder of many types of aircraft of the late 1920's, designed this pusher type with the engine atop the wing. For his own use, he had an F-11 amphibian with twin-tandem engines. Speed boat king Gar Wood owned and flew an F-11A out of Miami, Florida. There was a seating arrangement for eight.

```
Engine . . . . . . . . . . . . . . . . . . . . . . . . . . . . . . Wright Cyclone, 525 hp
Span . . . . . . . . . . . . . . . . . . . . . . . . . . . . . . . . . . . . . . . . . . . . . . . . . 59'
Length . . . . . . . . . . . . . . . . . . . . . . . . . . . . . . . . . . . . . . . . . . . . 45'10"
Maximum Speed . . . . . . . . . . . . . . . . . . . . . . . . . . . . . . . . . . . 112 mph
Range . . . . . . . . . . . . . . . . . . . . . . . . . . . . . . . . . . . . . . . . . . . 400 miles
```

FRAKES MALLARD

1971

Frakes Aviation of northern California, near Santa Rosa, is in the process of developing a high class performer in this Mallard, once built by Grumman. The standard radial engines were removed and two turbo Pratt and Whitney PT6A-27 engines were installed. These engines were built by United Aircraft of Canada. There is no change in wing span or length from the standard G-73 Mallard, but it can carry ten passengers and a crew of two.

Engines .... 2 Pratt & Whitney PT6A-27
Cruising Speed .... 220 mph
Fuel Capacity .... 700 gals
Gross Weight ....14000 lbs
Range .... 1500 miles

GOODYEAR GA-2 DUCK

1958

Manufacturers of tires for autos, buses and aircraft, the name "Goodyear" is world renowned for its products; but few people realize that the aviation section of Goodyear also designed and built this single engine pusher amphibian. This three-place experimental plane was built to determine if enough demand existed to justify its production. The Goodyear Aviation Department also built lighter-than-air ships.

Engine . . . . Franklin, 145 hp
Span . . . . 36'
Length . . . . 26'
Cruising Speed . . . . 110 mph

GREAT LAKES

Information, including year of manufacture and technical data for this amphibian aircraft, could not be located.

GREAT LAKES XSG-1

1934

The name "Great Lakes Airplanes" is well known to all sportsman pilots in the late 1920's and early 1930's. Many flew the popular open cockpit biplane known as the 2T-1A, with an inline Cirrus engine. The XSG-1 was built for the U.S. Navy for scouting flights. It had space for a crew of two: pilot and observer.

```
Engine ....................... Pratt & Whitney Wasp, Jr., 400 hp
Span ............................. 35' (Upper & Lower Wings)
Length .............................................. 32'7"
Maximum Speed ..................................... 124 mph
```

GRUMMAN SA-16 ALBATROSS

1955

Originally designed for the U.S. Air Force for air sea rescue operations, the U.S. Navy and Coast Guard also operate the Albatros, and call it the UF-1. Twelve stretchers can be readied for ambulance operations or ten passengers can be placed aboard.

```
Engines ................................ 2 Wright, 1425 hp each
Span ........................................................ 80'
Length ................................................... 61'4"
Cruising Speed ...................................... 225 mph
Range ............................................. 2700 miles
```

GRUMMAN J2F DUCK

1934

The J2F Duck was designed for the U.S. Sea Services as a utility and photographic plane. It was known as a JF-2 by the U.S. Coast Guard and the JF-1 by the U.S. Navy. The JF-1 could carry four persons and could be catapulted from the deck of a cruiser. This was the type of craft the U.S. Navy was looking for after they watched the performance.

```
Engine ................................. Pratt & Whitney, 770 hp
Span  ................................................. 39'
Length ................................................. 33'
```

GRUMMAN G-21 GOOSE

1937

The G-21 Goose was the first twin amphibian to be built by the Grumman firm. First tested in 1937, the Goose proved that Grumman had designed a fine twin amphibian for executive or sport flying. During World War II the Goose was brought into military service. In the Army Air Force it was called the OA-9. The U.S. Navy and the RCAF also operated them. A total of 345 G-21s were built.

```
Engines . . . . . . . . . . . . . . . . . . . . . . . . . 2 Pratt & Whitney, 450 hp each
Span . . . . . . . . . . . . . . . . . . . . . . . . . . . . . . . . . . . . . . . . . . . . . . . . 49'
Length . . . . . . . . . . . . . . . . . . . . . . . . . . . . . . . . . . . . . . . . . . . . . 38'3"
Maximum Speed . . . . . . . . . . . . . . . . . . . . . . . . . . . . . . . . . . 190 mph
```

GRUMMAN G-73 MALLARD

1950

Flying over a resort area near the Grumman factory, this is the largest
of all the commercial type of amphibians that Grumman built. One
of the Mallards has been seen recently on a TV travel program in
Detroit when sportsmen take a charter flight into Canada.

```
Engines ........................ 2 Pratt & Whitney, 550 hp each
Span ................................................. 66'8"
Length ............................................... 48'4"
Cruising Speed ....................................... 180 mph
Range ............................................... 1380 miles
```

GRUMMAN G-65 TADPOLE

1946

Designed by David Thurston when he was an engineer at Grumman, the Tadpole was built during World War II with the hope that it would be ideal for the sportsman pilot after the war. There is room for two people. Later the Tadpole was completely dismantled and stored.

Engine .... Continental, 125 hp
Span .... 35'
Length .... 23'6"
Cruising Speed .... 110 mph
Fuel Capacity .... 40 gals
Range .... 450 miles

NX4182B

6·18161
9·18·46

GRUMMAN G-44 WIDGEON

1940

During 1940 Leroy Grumman and B. A. Gilles were at the controls on the first flight with the Widgeon. The plane was built entirely of metal. The U.S. Coast Guard operated the Widgeon and called it the J4F-1. During World War II a JF4-1 sank a German U-boat with depth charges off the Louisiana coast. Other companies operated Widgeons in South America and Europe. The price, FAF, was $30,000.

```
Engines ................................. 2 Ranger, 200 hp each
Span ................................................. 40'
Length ......................... ...................... 31'
Cruising Speed ...................,................. 142 mph
Maximum Speed ................................... 150 mph
```

IRELAND NEPTUNE N2B

1928

The Ireland firm was founded in 1926 by Bertram Work, who was president. The vice president was G. S. Ireland. This little, stubby pusher job is an early type with open cockpit. Later, the Neptune had an enclosed cabin. About 15 Neptunes were built.

```
Engine ................................. Wright Whirlwind, 230 hp
Span ......................................... 40' Upper Wing
                                             34' Lower Wing
Length ............................................... 31'
Cruising Speed ................................... 90 mph
Range ......................................... 405 miles
```

IRELAND P-2 PRIVATEER

1931

The P-2 Privateer was built during the dark years of the big depression. It was mostly operated as a sport airplane, and sold at a cost of about $5,550. It had a 110 hp Warner Scarab engine but could be fitted with a 125 hp Warner engine. There was room for two persons. The Irelands were built on Long Island, New York.

Engine .... Warner Scarab, 110 hp
Span .... 38'
Length .... 28'
Cruising Speed .... 78 mph
Maximum Speed .... 95 mph
Gross Weight .... 1965 lbs
Range .... 300 miles

ISLAND SPECTRA

1971

This amphibian is very unusual, since the engine is mounted way back in the tail section. At present, the designer, Mr. Leroy Lopresti, is seeking financial aid to build two flight test models of the Spectra. The research plane pictured above is powered by a 125 hp Lycoming engine, but other advanced Spectras will have a 310 hp engine. Having two seats, the later prototype will have seating for four persons. With the 310 hp engine, the Spectra will cruise at 217 mph; cruising range will be 1,200 miles.

Engine . . . . Lycoming, 125 hp
Span . . . . 32'8"
Length . . . . 27'10"

LAKE LA-4 BUCCANEER

1971

Remember the Colonial Skimmer? The Buccaneer is a direct relation of it, only the LA-4 has been completely modified in the manufacturing blueprints. Buccaneers have been sold to countries all over the world. The purchase of a Buccaneer brings the owner a complete course on a water rating free. There is a seating arrangement for five people.

Engine .... Lycoming, 200 hp
Span .... 38'
Length .... 24'11"
Fuel Capacity .... 55 gals
Cruising Speed .... 150 mph
Range .... 650 miles

LAWRENCE SPERRY "BAT BOAT"

1917

The Bat Boat is the only tri-wing amphibian ever built. It was designed by Lawrence Sperry, the son of Elmer Sperry, inventor of the aircraft gyroscope stabilizer, also known as "The Automatic Pilot." This little triplane carried a crew of three.

Engine . . . . Liberty, 370 hp
Span . . . . 48' (All three wings)
Length . . . . 31'6"

LOENING AIR YACHT

1927

This six-place "Flying Shoehorn," as it was called by the pilots who flew them, operated between Detroit, Michigan, and Milwaukee, Wisconsin, with stops at Lansing, Grand Rapids, Muskegon and over 85 miles of Lake Michigan to Wisconsin. The Air Yacht is a direct descendant of the U.S. Navy's OL-8 scout and observation plane and carried six passengers. The pilot sat in an open cockpit just back of the top wing.

Engine . . . . Wright Cyclone, 523 hp
Span . . . . 46'8"
Length . . . . 34'8½"

LOENING AIR YACHT K-85

1931

The Model K-85 was developed for airline type service. It had a 3-bladed propeller. The K-85 was a fine looking amphibian, but wasn't in as great demand as expected, because it was way ahead of its time. The craft has space for nine people, including the pilot. The plane was built in Bristol, Pennsylvania.

Engine . . . . Wright Cyclone, 525 hp
Span . . . . 46'8" (Both Wings)
Cruising Speed . . . . 107 mph
Range . . . . 500 miles

LOENING COA-1

1925

This was Grover Loening's first amphibian type aircraft. Before this, he designed and built land planes, such as the M-80 two-seater fighter. This job outflew other types of fighter planes. This COA-1 amphibian is pictured at Ford Airport, Dearborn, Michigan, the home of the Ford Motor Company. Notice the four-bladed club type of propeller. Shortly after, the Liberty powered job saw service with the U.S. Army air service with a three-bladed prop installed.

Engine .... Inverted Liberty, 400 hp
Span .... 45'
Length .... 34'8"

110

LOENING K-84 COMMUTER

1930

Designed by Grover Loening with the engine under the top wing, this four-seater amphibian was built by the Keystone Aircraft Firm near Philadelphia. Over 35 Commuters were built.

```
Engine .............................. Wright Whirlwind, 300 hp
Span ................................ 40' (Upper & Lower Wings)
Length ............................................... 32'1"
Cruising Speed ..................................... 105 mph
Maximum Speed ..................................... 130 mph
Fuel Capacity ....................................... 70 gals
Range ............................................. 550 miles
```

LOENING DUCKLING

Information, including year of manufacture and technical data for this amphibian aircraft, could not be located.

LOENING MONODUCK

1934

Built especially for the personal use of Grover Loening, the Monoduck seated four persons. It was a development of the earlier Commuter. Only one Monoduck was built. This amphibian was probably the grandpappy of today's single engine tractor type amphibian. Split flaps were used to improve take-off and climb performance.

Engine . . . . Wright Whirlwind, 300 hp
Span . . . . 42'
Length . . . . 32'1"
Cruising Speed . . . . 100 mph
Maximum Speed . . . . 135 mph
Range . . . . 200 miles

LOENING OA-2

1929

Almost identical to the single wheel XO-10, the OA-2 has a standard type of landing gear. Notice also that the hull has been extended to a shoehorn type of Loening, though it was built by Keystone Aircraft. All of the OA and OL types were designed by Grover Leoning. Eight of these OA-2s were built.

Engine .... Wright, 480 hp
Span .... 44'11"
Length .... 34'11"
Maximum Speed .... 112 mph

LOENING OL-9

1928

This was the U.S. Navy's high performer in the late 1920's as an observation and scouting amphibian. The OL-9 was a two-seater, carrying a pilot and observer. The OL-9 could be catapulted from a cruiser's deck. All OL types were built by the Keystone Aircraft Firm.

Engine . . . . Pratt & Whitney Wasp, 425 hp
Span . . . . 45' (Upper & Lower Wings)
Length . . . . 35'2¼"
Maximum Speed . . . . 124 mph
Range . . . . 650 miles

LOENING XO-10

1927

This unusual amphibian was designed by Grover Loening. The single landing gear retracts into the center of the hull. With the wing skids under the wings the XO handles just like being on water. The U.S. Army purchased the XO-10 to be used as an observation plane but soon after, it was scrapped. The XO-10 had a crew of two.

Engine . . . . Inverted Wright, 500 hp
Span . . . . 46'3" (Upper & Lower Wings)
Length . . . . 35'

LOENING XO2L-1

1932

The XO2L-1 was the final design of the old-style of shoehorn amphibians, though the XO2L-1 has more of a modern-type hull. Having a crew of two, the XO2L-1 operated off aircraft carriers and could be catapulted from cruisers, from which it was operated as an observation aircraft. Slight changes in the second version brought out the XO2L-2, with only 100 hp more than the XO2L-1. Wingspan for the XO2L-1 is 37 feet; length is 29'10". Wingspan for the XO2L-2 is the same, but the length is 33'3"

```
Engine .................................. Pratt & Whitney, 430 hp
Span ................................................... 37'
Length ............................................. 29'10"
Maximum Speed ....................................... 121 mph
```

124

LOENING XSL-1

1931

The XSL-1 was another amphibian type designed for the U.S. Navy. It looks like it was a single-seater job. The X was for experimental; S was the code name for scouting; and L was for the designer—Loening; the 1 was the model number.

```
Engine ....................................... Warner, 110 hp
Span ................................................. 31′
Length ............................................. 27′2″
Maximum Speed .................................. 100 mph
Fuel Capacity .................................... 20 gals
Gross Weight ................................... 1512 lbs
```

LOENING XSL-2

1932

This craft was designed for the U.S. Navy for operating from a submarine. The wings could be folded back when aboard ships or subs, so the XSL-2 could be stored in compact places. This "submarine plane" was used for scouting and observation. It seated one person.

```
Engine ........................... Menasco Buccaneer, 160 hp
Span ................................................. 31'
Length ............................................. 27'2"
Fuel Capacity ................................... 30 gals
```

LOENING XS2L

1935

This little biplane amphibian was built for the U.S. Navy but never got beyond the experimental stage. Although the XSL2 flew very well, only one was built.

```
Engine . . . . . . . . . . . . . . . . . . . . . . . . . . . . . . Pratt & Whitney, Jr., 400 hp
Span  . . . . . . . . . . . . . . . . . . . . . . . . . . . . . . . . . . . . . . . . . . . . . 34'6"
Length . . . . . . . . . . . . . . . . . . . . . . . . . . . . . . . . . . . . . . . . . . . . 29'5"
Gross Weight . . . . . . . . . . . . . . . . . . . . . . . . . . . . . . . . . . . 3737 lbs
Maximum Speed . . . . . . . . . . . . . . . . . . . . . . . . . . . . . . . . . 136 mph
```

MC KINNON G-21D SUPER GOOSE

1960

When Leroy Grumman designed the G-21 Goose, he never dreamed that his design would ever be made into a four-engine plane; but Mc-Kinnon Enterprises of Sandy, Oregon, had other ideas. The two original P & W engines were replaced with 4, 340 hp Lycoming engines. Fuel capacity was increased from 220 gallons to 337 gallons. Seating arrangement including the pilot is fourteen. This amphibian was sold to a firm in the country of Pakistan.

Engines .... 4 Lycoming, 340 hp each
Span .... 50'10"
Length .... 39'7"
Fuel Capacity .... 337 gals
Cruising Speed .... 205 mph
Range .... 600 miles

MC KINNON SUPER WIDGEON

1971

The newest addition in the air for McKinnon Enterprises amphibian conversions, is this G-44 Widgeon. The two original Ranger engines have been replaced with two 270 hp Lycoming engines. The Super Widgeon can get off water in ten seconds; also unique are the retracting wing floats. It has a seating arrangement for six persons.

Engines . . . . 2 Lycoming, 270 hp each
Span . . . . 42'
Length . . . . 31'
Cruising Speed . . . . 180 mph
Gross Weight . . . . 5500 lbs
Range . . . . 1000 miles
Fuel Capacity . . . . 180 gals

MC KINNON TURBO GOOSE

1970

The old Gray Goose still lives and has gained in strength. This is a version of the G-21 Goose that McKinnon Aircraft Fabricators put more pep into. It has a seating arrangement for nine to twelve people, including the pilot. It has a 15″ extension in the bow for radar, a dorsal fin, and auxiliary wing tanks.

```
Engines .................... 2 Pratt & Whitney Turboprop, 680 hp
Span ................................................... 50′
Length ............................................... 39′7″
Fuel Capacity ..................................... 586 gals
Gross Weight .................................... 12500 lbs
Range ............................................ 1600 miles
```

MARTIN PBM-5A MARINER

1948

Builders of the world famous China Clipper of the 1930s, the first attempt by the Martin Company to build an amphibious type proved successful. It was designed for the U.S. Navy as a patrol bomber and has provisions for rocket-assisted take-off. Carries a crew of nine or more.

Engines . . . . 2 Pratt & Whitney, 2100 hp each
Span . . . . 118'
Length . . . . 69'10"
Cruising Speed . . . . 147 mph
Range . . . . 2300 miles

NIAGARA

1934

This single engine pusher type was built near Buffalo, New York. The designer had built it very near the world famous Niagara Falls; what a name for an amphibian aircraft. The Niagara is believed to be a two seater.

```
Engine ........................................ LeBond, 60 hp
Span ...................................................... 36'
Length ................................................. 24'3"
Cruising Speed ...................................... 85 mph
Maximum Speed ...................................... 93 mph
Fuel Capacity ...................................... 10 gals
Gross Weight ....................................... 1039 lbs
```

PACE GANNETT

1959

About thirty Grumman G-44 Widgeons have been purchased by a new firm near Los Angeles, California—Pacific Aircraft Engineering Corp. They have completely restyled the Widgeon, with two 300 hp Radial Lycoming engines. The Gannett has been stressed for 6000 lbs gross weight. A high performer even on one engine, it carries six passengers.

```
Engines ......................... 2 Radial Lycoming, 300 hp each
Span ...................................................... 40'
Length ................................................... 31'1"
Cruising Speed ....................................... 170 mph
Maximum Speed ...................................... 190 mph
Fuel Capacity ........................................ 158 gals
Range .............................................. 1000 miles
```

REPUBLIC RC-3 SEABEA

1946

Builders of the famous P-47 Thunderbolt fighter of the Second World War, Republic's offering to post-war private flying was the Seabea. The single engine pusher was used by many flying fishermen. The door on the right side of the panel and in the nose of the plane made it easy to cast a fishing line into the lake. It seats three.

```
Engine ...................................... Franklin, 175 hp
Span ............................................... 36'
Length ........................................... 26'6"
Cruising Speed ................................. 105 mph
Range ........................................ 420 miles
```

ROCHEVILLE TERN

1929

This very unusual twin-hull amphibian was built near Los Angeles, California, for photographic exploration in Alaska and Greenland. The two canopies on the leading edge of the wings have cameras inside. The Tern was a safe plane when it came to landing on open sea, since the cockpit was built high for the purpose of avoiding hidden shoals. The Tern carried enough fuel for ten hours of flight.

Engine . . . . Pratt & Whitney Wasp, Jr., 500 hp
Cruising Speed . . . . 165 mph

146

SCWEIZER TEAL TSC-1A

1970

The Colonial Skimmer Amphibian also was designed by Mr. David Thurston in the late 1940's. The entire structure is of aluminum alloy. It is a big favorite for sportsman pilots. The Teal is also built as a seaplane. It carries two.

```
Engine ....................................... Lycoming, 150 hp
Span ................................................. 31'11"
Length ................................................ 23'7"
Cruising Speed ...................................... 108 mph
Fuel Capacity ....................................... 65 gals
Range ............................................. 700 miles
```

SEVERSKY SEV-3

1933

The name Seversky stood out big with the U.S. Army Air Corps since the Seversky P-35 was their top pursuit plane of the 1930's. Major Seversky designed this SEV-3 amphibian, also, and had it built at the Edo Aircraft Float Firm. This plane still holds the record as the fastest amphibian ever built. It was clocked at the Cleveland National Air Races as it sped past the crowd doing well over 250 mph. It carried three persons.

```
Engine .............................. Wright Whirlwind, 420 hp
Span ................................................. 36'
Length ............................................. 25'8"
```

SIKORSKY S-34

1927

The first attempt by the Sikorsky Company to build an amphibian wasn't too satisfactory; but this S-34 with two Wright J-4 engines could fly one hour on one engine. Also, the S-34 was built to lift a payload of 2400 lbs. The end came to the S-34 when on June 1, 1927, the plane, with Mr. Igor Sikorsky, a former navy pilot and a mechanic, were on a test flight. She stalled out at 800 feet and nosed into the water near College Point, New York. All were shaken up, but unhurt.

Engines .... 2 Wright, J4

SIKORSKY S-36

1927

Only five of these were built. The U.S. Navy acquired one; another was bought by Mrs. Frances Grayson, the niece of President Woodrow Wilson. Her purpose was to fly the Atlantic Ocean. After hiring a pilot, they took off on Christmas Day, 1927. They were never heard of again. The craft was an eight seater, including pilot and co-pilot. Pan American Airways operated S-36s in South America.

Span . . . . 72'

SIKORSKY S-38B

1928

The pride of Mr. Igor Sikorsky, the S-38B was the first amphibian to fly new routes to South American countries by Pan American Airways. One S-38B was flown by Charles Lindbergh for the new routes. The U.S. Army Air Corps bought several and referred to them as the C-6A. The movie-making explorers, Oso and Martin Johnson, bought an S-38 to fly them around Borneo and Africa. Several airlines operated them. The plane seated eight.

```
Engines . . . . . . . . . . . . . . . . . . 2 Pratt & Whitney Wasps, 425 hp each
Span . . . . . . . . . . . . . . . . . . . . . . . . . . . . . . . . . . . . 71'8" Upper Wing
                                                              36' Lower Wing
Length . . . . . . . . . . . . . . . . . . . . . . . . . . . . . . . . . . . . . . . . . . 40'8"
Cruising Speed . . . . . . . . . . . . . . . . . . . . . . . . . . . . . . . . . 110 mph
Range . . . . . . . . . . . . . . . . . . . . . . . . . . . . . . . . . . . . . . . 750 miles
```

SIKORSKY S-39A

1929

The first try at a scaled-down version of the S-38B, was this Cirrus-powered twin engine. This was designed by Igor Sikorsky. The first flight for this twin, was December, 1929. Engine failure on the third flight caused a complete total.

Engines . . . . 2 Cirrus, 115 hp each

SIKORSKY S-39B

1930

The S-39A was flown during the National Air Tour of 1930, where it placed 18th. Many pilot sportsmen preferred the S-39 for going into Canada to fish or hunt. It seated five. At least one was operated by the Civil Air Patrol during World War II. The S-39B also saw safari service with Osa and Martin Johnson in Borneo and Africa. An S-39 is on display at the Connecticut Historical Museum, Windsor Locks Airport.

```
Engine ......................... Pratt & Whitney Wasp, Jr., 300 hp
Span ................................................. 52'
Length .............................................. 32'32"
Cruising Speed ...................................... 100 mph
```

SIKORSKY S-40

1931

The S-40 was the world's largest four engine amphibian. Because of all the struts, Charles Lindbergh called it "The Flying Forest." The S-40 flew to Washington, D.C., to be christened "The American Clipper" by the wife of President Herbert Hoover. Later Pan American Airways operated the S-40 on their South American routes. It could carry forty passengers.

```
Engines . . . . . . . . . . . . . . . . . 4 Pratt & Whitney Hornet, 575 hp each
Span . . . . . . . . . . . . . . . . . . . . . . . . . . . . . . . . . . . . . . . . . . . . . . . . . 114'
Length . . . . . . . . . . . . . . . . . . . . . . . . . . . . . . . . . . . . . . . . . . . . 76'8"
Cruising Speed . . . . . . . . . . . . . . . . . . . . . . . . . . . . . . . . . . . 117 mph
Gross Weight . . . . . . . . . . . . . . . . . . . . . . . . . . . . . . . . . . . . . 17 tons
Range . . . . . . . . . . . . . . . . . . . . . . . . . . . . . . . . . . . . . . . . . . 500 miles
```

SIKORSKY S-41

1932

The S-41 was the last of the big twin-boom amphibians built for Pan American Airways. Although there is no mention of the S-41 in two books on the history of Sikorsky, this big job helped Pan American Airways along. The craft could carry fifteen passengers.

```
Engines . . . . . . . . . . . . . . . . . . Pratt & Whitney Hornet, 575 hp each
Span . . . . . . . . . . . . . . . . . . . . . . . . . . . . . . . . . . . . . . . . . . . . . . 78'9¼"
Length . . . . . . . . . . . . . . . . . . . . . . . . . . . . . . . . . . . . . . . . . . . . . 45'2"
Cruising Speed . . . . . . . . . . . . . . . . . . . . . . . . . . . . . . . . . . . . 115 mph
Fuel Capacity . . . . . . . . . . . . . . . . . . . . . . . . . . . . . . . . . . . . 520 gals
```

164

SIKORSKY S-43

1935

In 1935, this was Sikorsky's latest design. A high-speed, long-range amphibian, it was ideal for airline operation. The first buyer was Pan American Airways. It has a seating arrangement for 25 passengers and performed very well in flight; at least one S-43 is still in existence.

Engines . . . . 2 Pratt & Whitney Hornet, 750 hp each
Span . . . . 84'
Length . . . . 50'5"
Cruising Speed . . . . 167 mph
Maximum Speed . . . . 187 mph

SIKORSKY S-61N

1969

The world's first amphibian helicopter built for airline operation and delivered to several foreign firms, the pictured craft is operated by San Francisco and Oakland Airlines around the Bay Area. It can carry twenty-six passengers. A Malaysian oil company operates an S-61N for off-shore oil work.

Engines .... 2 General Electric Turbo
Rotor Diameter .... 62'
Length .... 59'4"
Cruising Speed .... 140 mph
Range .... 480 miles

SIKORSKY S-62

1969

This single turbine helicopter is the first amphibious type of helicopter with flying boat type hull. Picked by the U.S. Coast Guard for rescue work and utility operations, it carries a crew of two and eleven passengers. It is operated by airlines and off-shore oil companies.

Engine .... General Electric Turbine, 1250 hp
Rotor Diameter .... 53'
Length .... 44'7"
Cruising Speed .... 98 mph
Range .... 474 miles

SIKORSKY XPS-1

1929

The civilian version of this craft is the S-36, but slight changes were made for this U.S. Navy patrol plane. The crew had a breezy flight in the three open cockpits. This picture was taken at Roosevelt Field, Long Island, New York, where Charles A. Lindbergh took off in the "Spirit of St. Louis" for Paris.

```
Engines . . . . . . . . . . . . . . . . . . . . . . . . . . . . . . . . . . 2 Wright, 220 hp each
Span . . . . . . . . . . . . . . . . . . . . . . . . . . . . . . . . . . . . . . . 71' Upper Wing
                                                              36' Lower Wing
Length . . . . . . . . . . . . . . . . . . . . . . . . . . . . . . . . . . . . . . . . . . . . . 36'8"
Gross Weight . . . . . . . . . . . . . . . . . . . . . . . . . . . . . . . . . . . . 9885 lbs
Fuel Capacity . . . . . . . . . . . . . . . . . . . . . . . . . . . . . . . . . . . 343 gals
Maximum Speed . . . . . . . . . . . . . . . . . . . . . . . . . . . . . . . 110 mph
Range . . . . . . . . . . . . . . . . . . . . . . . . . . . . . . . . . . . . . . . 1012 miles
```

SIKORSKY XP2S-1

1930

A plane without a name, this job was designed by the engineers at the Naval Aircraft Factory in Philadelphia, Pennsylvania, and was given to Sikorsky for manufacture. This biplane is a one-of-a-kind type. It had an engine in front and rear. The U.S. Navy operated their XP2S-1 as a patrol bomber.

Engines . . . . 2 Pratt & Whitney Wasp, 450 hp each
Span . . . . 56' (Upper & Lower Wings)
Length . . . . 44'1"
Cruising Speed . . . . under 100 mph
Range . . . . 300 miles

SIKORSKY XSS-2

1933

One of Sikorsky's rarest, and one-of-a-kind amphibians built for the U.S. Navy, this gull-wing job was operated as a scouting plane. The wings could be folded back to be stored in a small area. It has two cockpits: one for the pilot, the other for the observer. The engine looked a little large for this size of plane.

```
Engine ................................. Pratt & Whitney, 550 hp
Span ................................................... 42'
Gross Weight ....................................... 3940 lbs
```

SPENCER AIR CAR

1970

Another P. H. Spencer design is known as the "Air Car." Its first flight was at Chino Airport near Los Angeles, California, in May, 1970. This plane was built in a two-car garage at Mr. Spencer's house. Col. Anderson, a friend of Mr. Spencer, did a lot of work on the Air Car. It has a seating arrangement for four people.

Engine . . . . Lycoming, 260 hp
Span . . . . 37'4"
Length . . . . 26'5"
Cruising Speed . . . . 135 mph
Range . . . . 700 miles

SPENCER-LARSEN SL-12C

1939

Very unique in design, this pusher-type amphibian has the engine inside the hull and the prop driven through a gear transmission system that contains two vertical shafts, a flexible spline drive between the engine and transmission lines. Also the wing floats have the wheels in the floats that tilt backwards for water landings. The firm was headed by V. A. Larsen and P. H. Spencer, both veteran designers of fine aircraft. The SL-12C is a two-seater.

Engine .... Menasco, 125 hp
Span .... 40'
Length .... 26'1¼"
Cruising Speed .... 111 mph
Range .... 450 miles

STINSON A

1931

Most pilots that know about Stinsons remember the "A" type of airplane as a low wing, speedy trimotor. But the first "A" is this twin-engine amphibian that resembled the S-38B Sikorsky. This Stinson is a little smaller than the S-38 and wasn't very satisfactory in flight. It has a seating arrangement for five persons. The propellors are Hamilton standard.

```
Engines . . . . . . . . . . . . . . . . . . . . . . . . . . . . . 2 Lycoming, 215 hp each
Fuel Capacity . . . . . . . . . . . . . . . . . . . . . . . . . . . . . . . . . . . . 108 gals
```

STOUT

Information, including year of manufacture and technical data for this amphibian aircraft, could not be located.

4283-5-12-27

TOWLE TA-3

1930

Towle first came out with the TA-2, which had two Packard Diesels, but was only a seaplane. This TA-3, powered by two Packard Diesels, was the first to come out with an all metal hull in the U.S.A. The last report showed the TA-3 was used to haul whiskey from Canada to the U.S.A. by its final owners. Later it sank in the Detroit River.

```
Engines ........................ 2 Packard Diesel, 225 hp each
Span ................................................ 56'
Length ............................................. 42'
Cruising Speed ................................. 100 mph
Maximum Speed ............................... 124 mph
```

186

UNITED CONSULTANT TWIN BEA

1969

Developed from the Republic Seabea of 1946, which was a single-engine pusher amphibian, into a twin-engine tractor type, having an improved higher cruising speed, the Twin Bea can carry five people. United Consultant Corp. is still converting the original Seabea at their base in Massachusetts. The original Seabea was three feet shorter in fuselage length.

Engines .... 2 Lycoming, 180 hp each
Span .... 43'
Length .... 27'11"
Cruising Speed .... 135 mph

VOLMER VJ-22 SPORTSMAN

1958

Designed and built by Volmer Jensen, the "Chubasco," as Mr. Jensen calls the VJ-22, can be constructed from plans offered by Volmer to amateur builders that want a light amphibian two-place. The "Chubasco" has been all over the United States and Central America. A 125 hp Lycoming engine was installed by a Canadian that bought a set of plans from Mr. Jensen.

Engine .... Continental, 85 hp
Span .... 36'6"
Length .... 24'
Cruising Speed .... 85 mph
Range .... 300 miles